Follow That Map!
A First Look at Mapping Skills

Scot Ritchie

Kids Can Press

To my friends and family around the world — S.R.

Kids Can Press gratefully acknowledges the financial support of the Government of Ontario, through the Ontario Media Development Corporation; the Ontario Arts Council; the Canada Council for the Arts; and the Government of Canada, through the CBF, for our publishing activity.

Published in Canada and the U.S. by Kids Can Press Ltd.
25 Dockside Drive, Toronto, ON M5A 0B5

Kids Can Press is a Corus Entertainment Inc. company

www.kidscanpress.com

Edited by Lisa Tedesco
Designed by Julia Naimska and Kathleen Gray

Printed and bound in Malaysia in 7/2017 by Tien Wah Press (Pte.) Ltd.

CM 09 20 19 18 17 16 15 14 13 12 11 10 9
CM PA 09 0 9 8 7 6 5

Library and Archives Canada Cataloguing in Publication

Ritchie, Scot
    Follow that map! : a first book of mapping skills / written and illustrated by Scot Ritchie.

Includes index.
ISBN 978-1-55453-274-2 (bound)
ISBN 978-1-55453-275-9 (pbk.)

1. Map reading—Juvenile literature. 2. Maps—Juvenile literature. I. Title.

GA105.6.R58 2009   j912.01'4   C2008-903989-0

Contents

Getting Started

Do you know how to find a hidden treasure? Do you know how far your house is from the candy store? Do you know the way to your favorite ride at the amusement park? It's easy! Join the friends below and follow that map!

A map is a drawing that tells you about a place. There are many different parts to a map. This map explains what some of those parts are.

The **compass rose** on a map will always point north. Some compass roses show all four cardinal directions — north, south, east and west.

The **scale bar** on a map helps you measure distance. The line on this map shows that Sally is 16 km (10 mi.) from the landmark.

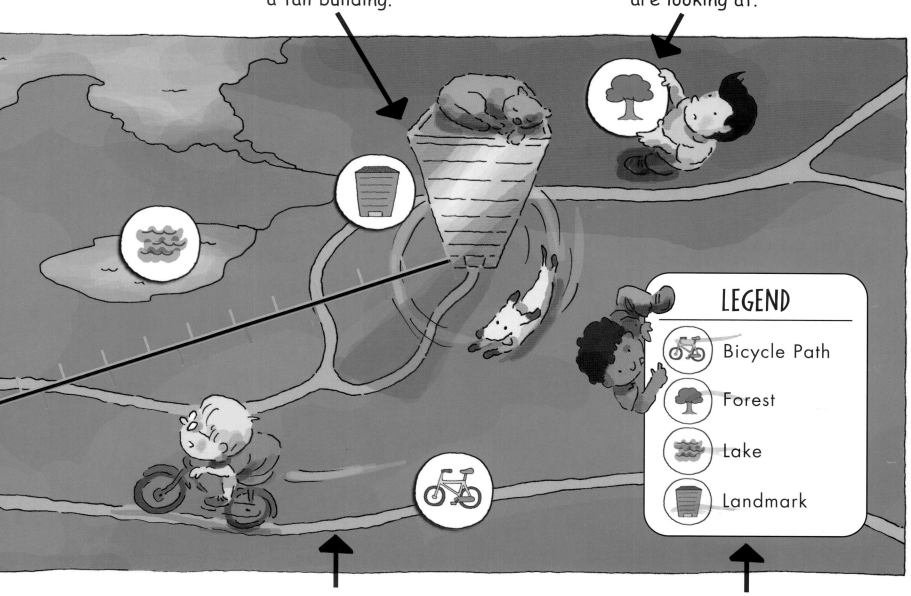

A **landmark** is something that is easy to find, like a tall building.

A **symbol** on a map is a small drawing that tells you what you are looking at.

LEGEND

🚲 Bicycle Path

🌳 Forest

〰️ Lake

🗑 Landmark

Some maps show paths or **routes** that help you find your way.

Most maps have a **legend** or **key**. The legend explains what all the symbols on the map mean.

One Sunny Day ...

Sally and her friends are playing in her backyard. Pedro notices that Sally's dog, Max, and her cat, Ollie, are missing.

Where have Max and Ollie gone? The five friends decide to find out!

First Stop ...

Yulee has an idea! Maybe Max and Ollie are visiting their favorite places in the neighborhood. The children spread out and start their search.

Can you find the symbol for the park on the legend and on the map?

Maps use symbols to help you find important places, such as the hospital, your school or your home. The symbols are explained on a legend or key.

LEGEND

- Candy Store
- Library
- Park
- Sally's House

Follow That Trail ...

Sally thinks going to the park next is a good idea. She takes Max for walks in the park every day. The children will follow the route from start to finish.

Keep your eyes open. Somebody is going the wrong way. Who is it?

A map can show you which path to follow so you won't get lost. The route on this map is colored yellow and marked with red arrows.

In the City ...

No luck on the trail. Yulee suggests going to the city zoo. Maybe Max and Ollie are visiting the animals.

Martin is getting close to the zoo. Which direction is he running?

The compass rose on a map shows you directions such as north, south, east and west.

5 km
0 1 2 3 4 5

3 miles
0 1 2 3

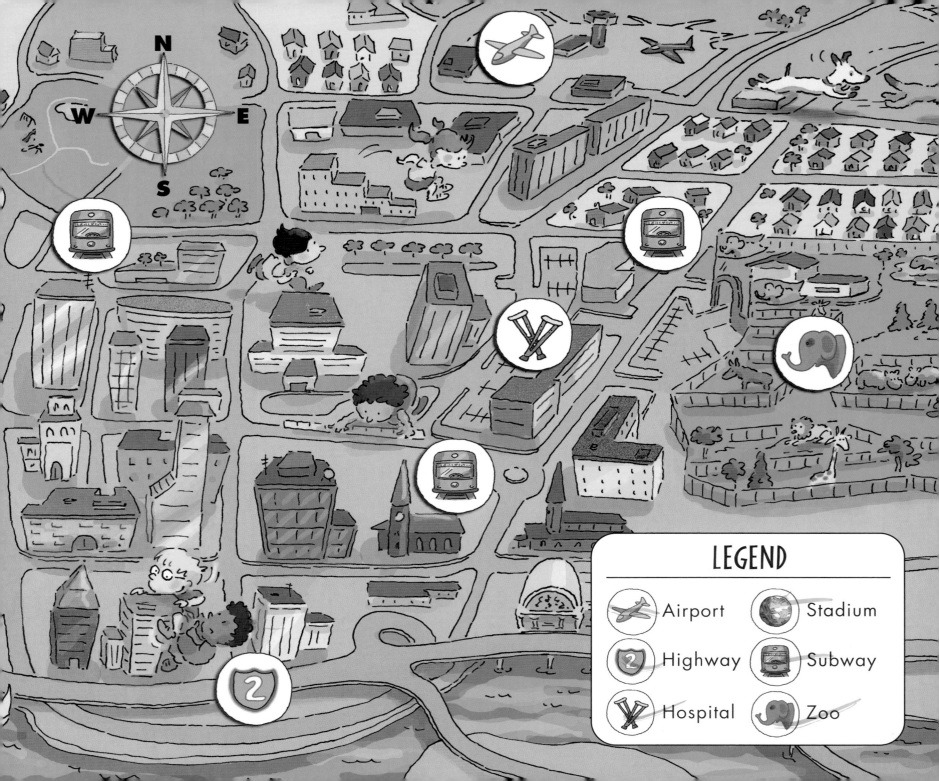

LEGEND

✈	Airport	🌐	Stadium
②	Highway	🚈	Subway
🩼	Hospital	🐘	Zoo

Off to the Country ...

Still no sign of Max and Ollie. Pedro has a hunch. Maybe they have left town. The children leave the city and search the countryside.

How far is Martin from the tractor?
(Hint: Measure from the tip of Martin's nose to the big wheel on the tractor.)

You can use the scale bar on a map to see how far away something really is. The scale bar on this map shows you how to measure distance using either kilometers or miles.

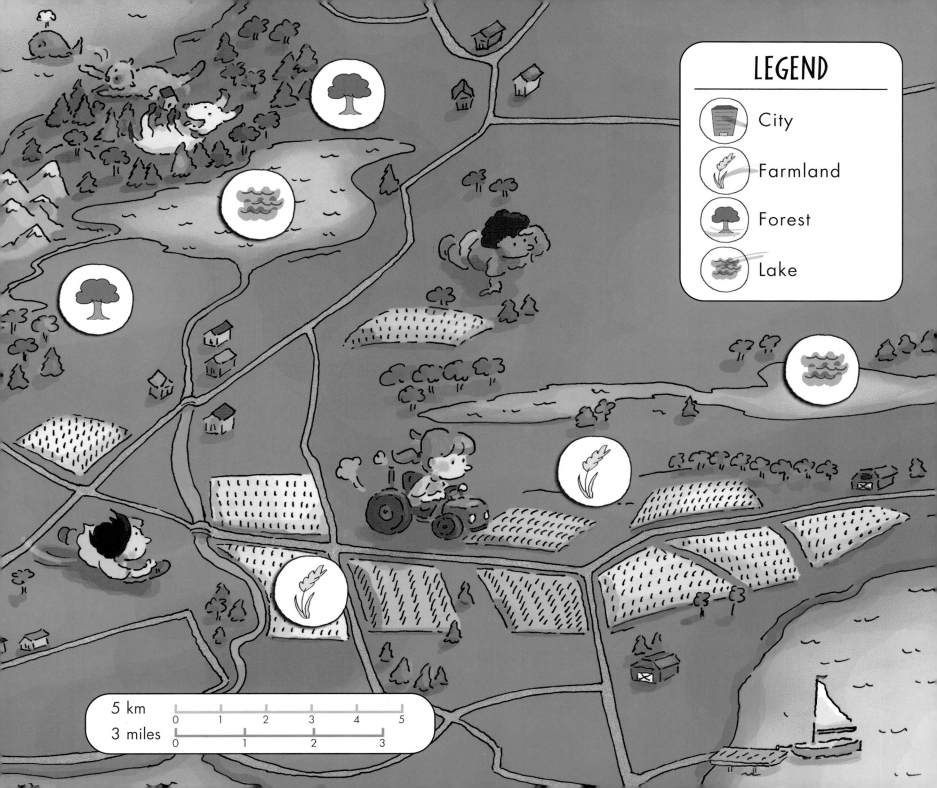

LEGEND

- 🏢 City
- 🌾 Farmland
- 🌳 Forest
- 〰️ Lake

5 km 0 1 2 3 4 5

3 miles 0 1 2 3

Hot, Cold, Wet, Dry ...

Look out! The weather is changing. Good thing Martin brought an umbrella. The children hope that Max and Ollie aren't getting too wet.

What's the weather like where Max and Ollie are?

A weather map is different from other kinds of maps. It can show how warm a place is or whether it is raining somewhere.

LEGEND

Cloudy

Lightning

Rainy

Sunny

X Marks the Spot ...

Once the weather clears and the children are all dried off, Nick suggests a boat ride to the mysterious island. Sally finds a treasure map, but the children don't find Max and Ollie.

Follow the friends to their big surprise!

A treasure map is a kind of puzzle. X marks the spot where you'll find treasure!

Go 7 steps east.
Cross Serpent
Bridge. Jump on 8
stepping stones, but
STOP before
Alligator Beach.
Go south to find
the treasure.
X marks the spot!

Up, Down, All Around ...

Tickets to Playland! What a great treasure. The children hop on the train and they're on their way.

How many mountains do they travel over on the train ride?

A topographical map shows the natural features of a landscape. You can use this kind of map to find rolling hills, low-lying lakes or high mountains.

LEGEND

- Cliff
- Mountain
- Plateau
- Volcano

All Fun and Games ...

Sally and Pedro have a great time riding the Ferris wheel. They can see everything for miles around. Well, maybe not everything ... look who's right in front of them!

The Ferris wheel is tall, but there's a landmark that's even taller. Can you find it on the legend and the map?

A landmark is something that is easy to find. It might be a tall statue, an important building or a funny-looking tree.

LEGEND

- ✕ Food
- 🐐 Petting Zoo
- 🗼 The Spinner
- 🚻 Washrooms

Around the World ...

The five friends had so much fun at Playland, they almost forgot about Max and Ollie. Where in the world could they be?

What part of the world would you go to to find Max and Ollie?

Earth is shaped like an orange. In order to show the whole world at once, a mapmaker "peels" Earth's surface just like an orange and lays it down flat. On a flat map, curved gridlines help remind you of Earth's real shape.

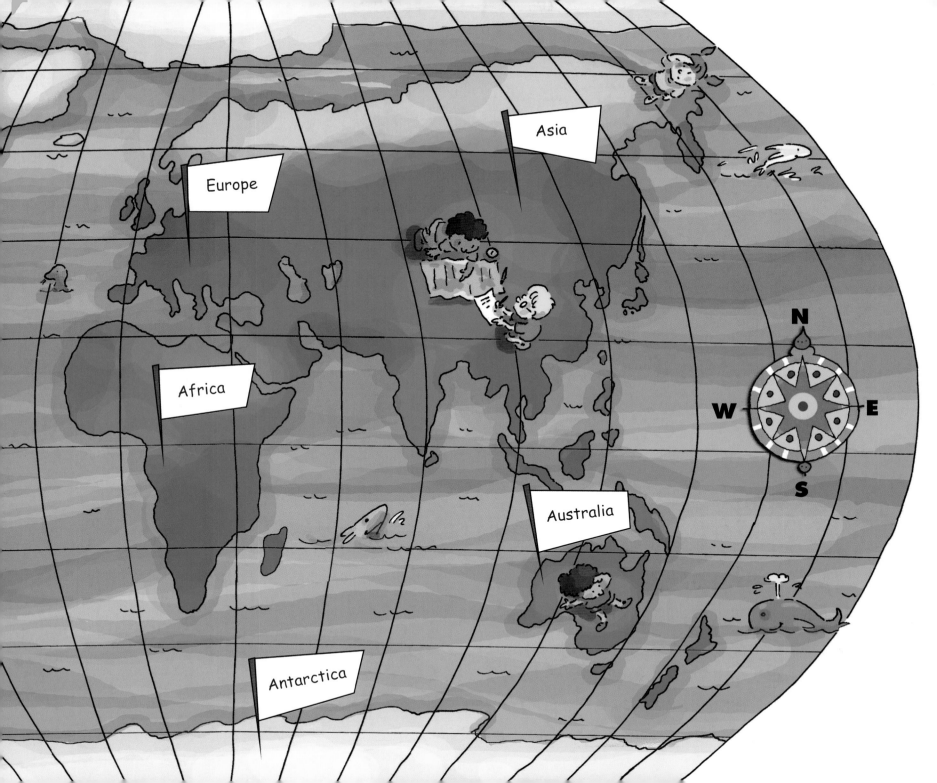

Blast Off ...

Max and Ollie could be anywhere in the universe. And it's almost dinner time. There's just enough time to check each of the planets.

Which planet is Yulee heading to next?

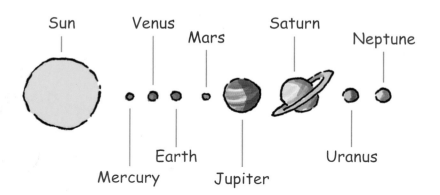

Sun   Venus   Mars   Saturn   Neptune

Mercury   Earth   Jupiter   Uranus

You can use a telescope to look at stars and even planets, but you will never see all the planets at once. This map lets you imagine what the planets would look like if they were all lined up together.

Home Again ...

Dinner time! The adventure is over for today. But where are Max and Ollie? There they are, sleeping under the big tree. Have they been there all afternoon?

Let's do this again tomorrow!

Create Your Own Map

Here's a map of Sally's bedroom.

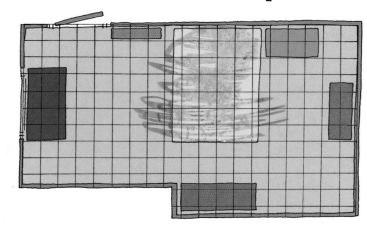

You can make a map just like Sally's by following these steps:

Step 1: Find a sheet of graph paper and a pencil. If you don't have graph paper, make your own by using a ruler and a pencil to divide a piece of plain paper into equal squares.

Step 2: Measure your room using your footsteps. Each step you take will equal one square on your graph paper. Walk the length and width of your room and record the number of footsteps.

Step 3: Use the measurements you recorded to draw the outline of your room on the graph paper. Remember, each square equals one footstep.

Step 4: Using your footsteps again, measure the length and width of each piece of furniture in your room and add them to your map. Place them in the same location as they appear in your room. Don't forget to include any doors and windows on your map, too.

Step 5: Use markers or pencil crayons to color each piece of furniture and create a legend or key to explain the colors.

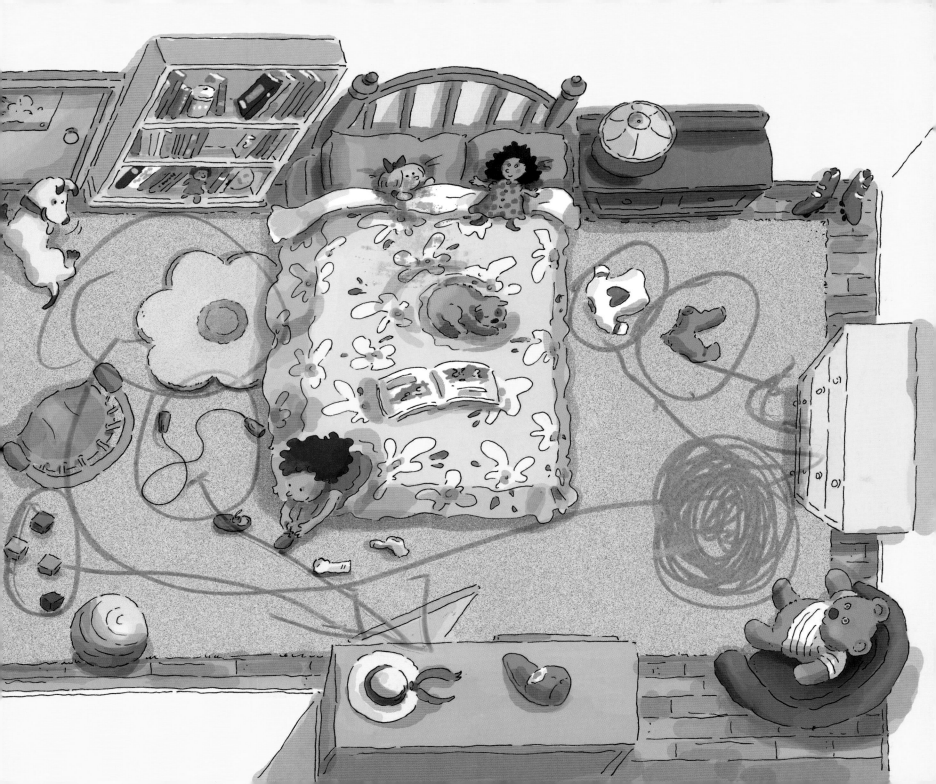

Index